Read and Do Science
ROCKS

Written by Melinda Lilly

Photos by Scott M. Thompson

Design by Elizabeth Bender

Educational Consultants

Kimberly Weiner, Ed.D

Betty Carter, Ed.D

Maria Czech, Ph.D
California State University Northridge

Rourke
Publishing LLC

Vero Beach, Florida 32964

Before You Read This Book

Think about these facts:

1. What is a rock?

2. How do you think rocks are made?

The experiments in this book should be undertaken with adult supervision.

For Lyra

—S. T.

The photos on pages 8, 9a, 11, and 17a are courtesy of the National Park Service.

Thank you to Paul David Numer of Devil's Punchbowl Nature Center.

Library of Congress Cataloging-in-Publication Data

Lilly, Melinda
  Rocks / Lilly, Melinda.
      p. cm. -- (Read and do science)
  ISBN 1-59515-404-3 (hardcover)

Printed in the USA

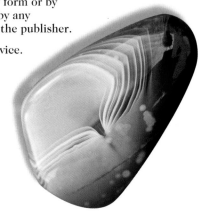

Table of Contents

What can be as old as the hills
or as young as this minute?

Not your grandpa!

ROCKS!

Land may seem as though it never changes. However, your backyard may once have been a desert, a rain forest, a swamp, or more. A dinosaur may have roamed where you now climb on a slide.

5

Sedimentary Rocks

Sedimentary rocks tell the history of the land. They are made of soil and other materials brought by water, wind, and ice. Each time the land changes it makes a new layer.

yum!

The layers make some sedimentary rocks look like slices of layer cake.

6

Squeeze the layers together for millions of years and they become sedimentary rocks.

Igneous Rocks

Some rocks start out as hot **molten rock,** flowing like syrup. They can burst out of a volcano or remain trapped deep in the earth.

When molten rock cools and hardens it becomes **igneous** rock.

Metamorphic Rocks

Burst out of a volcano? That's nothing!

It's hair-raising with what some rocks go through!

Earthquakes and other forces may squish and fold them. Hot liquids may splash them until they *almost* become molten rock. Some go through it all!

These rocks may have originally been igneous or sedimentary. The heat and stress change them, and they become **metamorphic** rocks.

Which Description Best Describes Which Type of Rock?

1. Stacked like pancakes

2. Made of rock that bubbles and bakes

3. Squeezed and folded when the earth quakes

A. Sedimentary

B. Metamorphic

C. Igneous

Answers: 1 A, 2 C, 3 B

Follow this recipe to make pretend rocks!

Rock Recipe

What You Need:
- 1 1/2 cups flour
- 1/2 cup pebbles or gravel
- 1 cup sand
- 1/4 cup rock salt
- 3 tablespoons alum (at the grocery store on the spice shelf)
- 3/4 cup water
- A big bowl
- A tablespoon

If you were making real rocks, **minerals** would be your ingredients. A mineral used in this recipe is **halite,** which is natural rock salt.

Put everything in the bowl. Mix.

Ick! It's not like cookie dough!

Grab a handful of rock dough.

Put it under a mountain. Wait a million years for the earth to shape it into a rock.

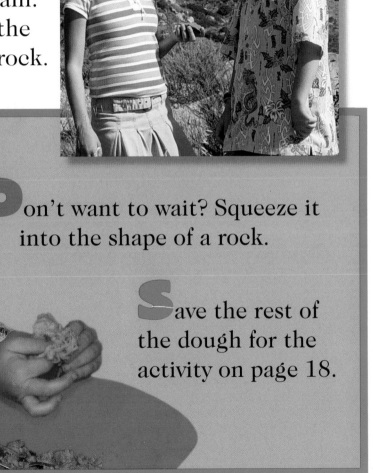

Don't want to wait? Squeeze it into the shape of a rock.

Save the rest of the dough for the activity on page 18.

Set your rock aside. Check it in a week to see if it's as hard as a rock.

How is a real rock like yours?

leaf fossil

Some rocks have **fossils** or gems inside. **Paleontologists** study fossils to learn about animals and plants of long ago.

shell fossils

Hide pretend fossils and gems, and then dig for them!

Dig

What You Need:
- Rock dough (recipe on page 13)
- Chicken bones
- Shells
- Fake gems
- At least 25 pounds (11.3 kilograms) of clean sand
- A plastic tub or other container
- Plastic shovels

Hide bones, shells, or gems inside each ball of rock dough.

Wait two days. Your rocks should be slightly soft. You need to be able to open them with your hands.

Have an adult pour sand into the plastic tub.

Hide the rocks.

Dig in!

Pry open the rocks.

Buried treasure!

What other secrets do rocks contain?

Geologists study them to learn what the world was like long ago. Rocks also reveal the ingredients that make up the earth. It's some recipe!

Glossary

erosion (ih ROW zhun) — the wearing away of land by water, ice, wind, or other forces

fossils (FOS ilz) —anything remaining of animals or plants that lived in ancient times

geologists (jee ALL oh jists) — scientists who study the history and make-up of the earth

halite (HAL iet) — natural rock salt mineral

igneous (IG nee us) — rock made by great heat in the earth

metamorphic (met ah MAR fik) —rock that has changed its form

minerals (MIN er alz) — natural substances with specific chemical make-ups, minerals are the building blocks of rocks

molten rock (MOAL ten ROK) — rock that is so hot it has melted and is a liquid

paleontologists (pay lee on TALL oh jists) — scientists who study ancient life

sedimentary (sed ih MEN tah ree) — rock that is formed of dirt and other material left by wind, water, or ice

Take It Further: Water Erosion

Learn how water changes the landscape by washing some of it away. Shape the sand in the plastic tub into hills and valleys. Put rocks, shells, and other items in your landscape.

Using a large spray bottle or a hose with a spray attachment, spray water on your landscape as rain. Watch how the hills and valleys change through **erosion.**

What happens to the sand underneath the rocks and other items? How will the landscape erode if you put ice on the sand instead of water?

Think About It!

1. Hawaii was formed by volcanoes. Could you expect to find a lot of metamorphic, igneous, or sedimentary rocks in Hawaii?

2. If you wanted to go fossil hunting, would you look for igneous, metamorphic, or sedimentary rocks?

3. Please pass the halite! There are other types of natural salt besides rock salt. Where is another place in nature that you could find salt?

Index